MENTAL HEALTH

PERSONALITIES

PERSONALITY DISORDERS, MENTAL DISORDERS & PSYCHOTIC DISORDERS

Second Edition

CAROL FRANKLIN

© 2015

COPYRIGHT NOTICE

DISCLAIMER

Although the author and publisher have made every effort to ensure that the information in this book was correct at press time, the author and publisher do not assume and hereby disclaim any liability to any party for any loss, damage, or disruption caused by errors or omissions, whether such errors or omissions result from negligence, accident, or any other cause.

This book is not intended as a substitute for the medical advice of physicians. The reader should regularly consult a physician in matters relating to his/her health and particularly with respect to any symptoms that may require diagnosis or medical attention.

TABLE OF CONTENTS

INTRODUCTION

Everyone has their own personality; it is what makes you unique. Personalities are, to some extent shaped by your upbringing. Until the end of the 19th century it was believed that your personality was set as a young person and could not be changed. However, it is now apparent that your personality will evolve over time, there are many ways you can help yourself to improve your personality and become have, what is seen as; a good personality. This is generally defined as a personality which is appealing to others and makes you likeable, interesting and enjoyable to be with. Whilst there are steps which can be taken to improve your personality this does not necessarily help those with a personality disorder.

The cause of a personality disorder is still being researched. There is some genetic evidence to suggest that obsessive compulsive disorders are caused by an abnormality in your genes; which would make it very difficult, if not impossible to change. The majority of research points towards environmental factors causing, or increasing the likelihood of developing a disorder, such as:

- Abuse or neglect as a child
- Family history of personality disorders
- Unstable family life, or even simply a chaotic family life during your early years
- Significant trauma; this is usually an incident when you are young but significant trauma can affect adults as well.

Personality disorders have, historically, been classed as a category of mental disorders. However, as governments have added regulations allowing those of unsound mind; namely a threat to themselves or others, to be incarcerated, it has become essential to decide when a personality disorder is also a mental disorder. This is a difficult and complex subject and one that does not, yet, have a definitive answer.

Someone with a personality disorder will display long-term patterns of unhealthy, rigid behaviors and thoughts. The condition will cause significant impairment in a person's life, affecting many aspects including social, personal, and work. Perhaps the most obvious feature of these disorders is the noticeable negative effect they have on peoples' relationships with others. Someone with a personality disorder is likely to display some, or all of the following symptoms:

- Mood swings
- Extreme dependency on other people
- Difficulty controlling their response to any situation
- Angry outbursts
- Suspicious of others
- Difficulty maintaining a relationship due to constant conflict
- Struggle to make friends
- A need to be satisfied instantly
- Social isolation
- A love of themselves, above anything else.

Many people display some or all of these traits and do not have a personality disorder; this is because they are typically not diagnosed until you are in your 20s or 30s. Until this point you may have the symptoms but it will not be significantly impairing your everyday life. People who have personality disorders are not able to function in their lives as others can; this is because the behavioral patterns will be extreme and they will be unable to change them. There are treatment options but these disorders are very hard or sometimes even impossible to cure. More often than not, individuals refuse to believe that they have a disorder; which causes them to resist treatment.

CHAPTER 1: PERSONALITY TYPES

Katherine Briggs and Isabel Myers postulated that there are sixteen personality types. Their work was based upon research conducted by Carl Jung; the emphasis of this work was the belief that all humans have one dominant personality trait out of the four principle traits:

- Sensation
- Intuition
- Feeling
- Thinking

Briggs and Myers built on these initial findings to arrive at sixteen distinct personality types; their findings are still generally accepted today. Each personality is made up of one part of each of the following four criteria:

Extraverted (E) or Introverted (I) – Extraverts expend their energy outwards whilst introverts focus on their own, internal world.

Sensing (S) or Intuition (N) – Those who have a sensing personality will believe information that they receive from external sources, such as newspapers or the internet. People with an intuitive nature will rely on what they know themselves.

Thinking (T) or Feeling (F) – This is the decision making part of a person's make-up. Those who think tend to make decisions based on logic; feelers will base their movements on emotions.

Judging (J) or Perceiving (P) – Those who have the judging trait are likely to be highly organized and follow a set plan. People who tend to perceive are those which are more willing to go with the flow and improvise.

The sixteen personality types are briefly explained below:

ISTJ

People with this personality will tend to be quiet, serious and dependable. They will adopt a practical, matter-of-fact approach to life. They will usually look at everything from a logical viewpoint to decide what approach to take. They are then likely to work toward it steadily whilst refusing to be distracted. They will take great pleasure in keeping things organized; whether at work or at home. They will also place a high emphasis on traditions and loyalty.

ISFJ

Someone with this personality type will be quiet but friendly, particularly if you take the initiative in getting to know them. They are generally responsible and conscientious. If they take on a project they will remain committed until it has been achieved. They thrive on detail, always striving to be accurate. They also tend to be incredibly loyal and considerate with an excellent memory, particularly regarding specifics about people in their lives. This type of person will be overly concerned with how others feel. As such they will be constantly striving to create an orderly and harmonious environment; wherever they are.

INFJ

This type of person looks for the meaning in everything and makes connections through their ideas. They can become obsessed with wanting to understand what motivates people; this can make them very insightful individuals. They will usually have a firm set of beliefs and values which they will remain committed to, even under pressure. They also love to develop their own vision of how to improve life for everyone around them.

INTJ

Someone with this personality type likes to be original. Once an idea has formed they will have the necessary drive to ensure it is fully implemented; they will not stop until they achieve their goals. People with the INTJ personality type will quickly see patterns in external events; this will assist them with developing a long term perspective. They will always see a job through to the very end. They will always expect the best from both themselves and others; they usually have incredibly high standards of competence and performance.

ISTP

A person with this type of personality will generally be tolerant and flexible. They will usually be happy to observe until a problem appears; then they will act quickly to find the best possible solution. They are exceptionally good at analyzing large amounts of data and understanding what makes something work. Their logical approach leads them to be interested in cause and effect, whilst their organized approach places an emphasis on efficiency.

ISFP

This personality is generally quiet, friendly, very sensitive and usually kind to others, particularly those in need. They live in the moment, enjoying what is happening around them. They do not like to be rushed, preferring to work to their own schedule in their own space. Personal boundaries are important to them. They generally make excellent friends as they are loyal and committed; both to their beliefs and to people who are important to them. Wherever possible they will avoid conflicts and they will never force their opinions or values onto others.

INFP

This personality type tends to be idealistic and loyal. They constantly look outwards and want a life that is in keeping with their own values. They are always curious and will usually see an opportunity or possibilities before anyone else. This can often be used as a catalyst for creating and implementing new ideas. They are focused on people and love to help anyone understand themselves better and fulfill their potential. They are generally very accepting of others and their ideas, unless it threatens one of their core beliefs.

INTP

This personality type looks to develop a logical explanation for everything. They are generally withdrawn from society as they focus on theories and abstract possibilities, negating social interaction in the process. When in the room they will be quiet and will contain their thoughts and feelings, preferring to listen to others and use this information in their own theories. They are generally very flexible and adaptable and are exceptionally good at focusing on a problem and finding a workable solution, providing it is in association with a subject that interests them. They can be skeptical of others and, at times, immensely critical.

ESTP

People with this personality are incredibly flexible and tolerant. They prefer to see immediate results and will adapt their approach to achieve this. They are not generally interested in theories and conceptual explanations; generally preferring to act rather than think. Their focus is on the now; they are spontaneous and look to enjoy each moment, preferably in the company of like-minded individuals. They generally enjoy the good things in life and look after themselves and their friends.

ESFP

Someone with this personality type will be outgoing, friendly, and quick to accept others, no matter what their situation. They love life, being with people and enjoy the finer things in life. They are prepared to work with anyone to ensure things get done. They also possess a lot of common sense and always have a realistic approach to their work, preferring to make it fun whenever possible. They are likely to be very flexible and spontaneous, eager to meet new people and experience new things.

ENFP

Should you meet someone with this personality type they are likely to be enthusiastic and imaginative. To them, life is full of possibilities. They are very quick to connect information and events and make decisions on the conclusions they draw. They will then be confident proceeding on any path in-line with their findings. They do, however, require plenty of appreciation from others; they are quick to provide appreciation and support. They are generally very spontaneous and quick to try new things; often relying on their natural ability to improvise and their verbal fluency.

ENTP

This personality type is a quick thinker and will arrive at an ingenious solution to any problem which is probably not visible to others. They are highly alert and not afraid to voice their opinion when required. They are also surprisingly resourceful when dealing with new and challenging issues. They are also excellent at theorizing possibilities and then analyzing them strategically to decide whether it is a workable solution or not. They are generally very good at reading other people but do not like to stick to a routine, it is rare that they will do something the same way twice. Their attention span tends to be limited as they will quickly lose interest in one project or hobby and move onto a new one.

ESTJ

This type of person is immensely practical. They are realistic and will look at all the facts before quickly making a decision and then implementing it. They are excellent at organizing projects and motivating people to get things done. They will generally focus on getting results in the most efficient way possible and will always ensure the little details are taken care of. They have a well defined set of standards which they prefer to follow and like to see others following their lead. They can also be surprisingly forceful when looking to implement their latest plans.

ESFJ

People with this personality type are warm hearted, conscientious, and cooperative. They prefer to live and work in a harmonious environment and will do everything within their power to establish the right environment. They prefer to work with others and always want to complete tasks accurately and on time. They are exceptionally loyal to those who have earned their trust and will follow through on even the smallest of matters. They are generally very good at noticing what others need in their daily lives and will do what they can to make it happen. In return they like to be appreciated for who they are and for what they contribute.

ENFJ

This personality type is generally warm, empathetic and responsible. They are highly aware of the emotional needs of others and are usually able to see what motivates people. They are quick to see the potential in everyone and love helping others to reach their potential. They can often be seen to be the catalysts for growth within a group and on an individual level. People with this personality type will be sociable and loyal to those they trust.

ENTJ

This personality belongs to natural leaders; they are decisive and quick to make decisions, whilst being happy to assume a leadership role. They have a logical approach to life and can easily see which policies and procedures are inefficient. This allows them to develop and implement solutions to these issues. They are excellent at planning for the long term and will set goals along the way to ensure all targets are met. They like to stay up to date with all developments in their chosen field, normally enjoying expanding their horizons and sharing their knowledge with others. They can be incredibly forceful when persuading others to take part in their ventures.

There are many websites online which will provide a short, multiple choice test, to establish which personality type you are. Understanding your general traits and characteristics will assist you in knowing when you behavior is normal for your personality type and when it is extreme and liable to be classed as a personality disorder.

CHAPTER 2: PERSONALITY DISORDERS, MENTAL DISORDERS & PSYCHOTIC DISORDERS

It is important to understand the differences between personality disorders, mental disorders and psychotic disorders. You will already have read the introduction and understand a personality disorder may be a result of environment or genes. It is in essence an extreme version of normal reactions to stimuli, but the person with this disorder is unable to prevent the reaction or adjust their behavior to prevent it happening.

The following brief summary of mental and psychotic disorders will help you to understand the differences.

Mental Disorders

As with a personality disorder a mental disorder; or illness will affect your ability to function normally. It is likely to cause you considerably stress over the duration of the illness.

A mental disorder is classified as any medical condition which will disrupt a person's ability to relate to others and function normally. This is usually displayed through intense feelings and thoughts. A mental illness can affect anyone, although young adults and elderly people are more likely to suffer from this issue.

There are many causes of mental disorders, your upbringing or your genes can play a part but it can also be due to a traumatic injury or substance abuse. It is even possible to have a mental illness as a result of a parent's exposure to a virus while you are still in the womb. The good news is that the majority of mental illnesses can be treated with medication and therapy. Dieting and exercise can also help.

The most common mental disorders are:

- Severe Depression
- Bipolar Disorder
- Obsessive Compulsive Disorder
- Panic Disorder
- Post Traumatic Stress Disorder

Personality and psychotic disorders are often included under the umbrella of mental disorders; it is a fine line which many have argued over and few have provided a definitive explanation for.

Psychotic Disorders

These are defined as extreme versions of mental disorders with abnormal thinking and a lack of perception of what is real or not. People who suffer from psychotic disorders are likely to have delusions and hallucinations. A delusion is any kind of false belief and usually manifests as a paranoia that others are plotting against you or are trying to pass you secret messages. A hallucination is anything that you feel, see or hear which is not real but you believe is. This type of illness will reduce your ability to think clearly, function properly and even live a normal life. People who contract this type of illness will show a steady decline in the ability to relate to others, make good judgments, connect emotionally to anyone or anything; it is even possible their ability to communicate will diminish.

Psychotic disorders are treatable, again with medication and therapy; with the right care and medical attention it is possible to live a full and happy life.

Common psychotic disorders include:

Schizophrenia - This is an illness which changes the behavior and is usually accompanied by hallucinations and delusions. It must usually last longer than six months to be classified as Schizophrenia.

Schizoaffective Disorder – This is a variant of Schizophrenia; people who suffer from this have both Schizophrenia and a mood disorder; such as Bi-polar.

Schizophreniform – This is the name for anyone who displays the symptoms of Schizophrenia but the condition only lasts for between one and six months.

Delusional Disorder – Anyone suffering from this condition will believe that something is true, when it is not. This is a difficult one to treat as the sufferer will have a plausible delusion, based on a real life scenario. The delusions will persist for at least one month.

Shared psychotic Disorder – If one person becomes delusional it can sometimes be so convincing that their partner can start to believe the same delusion; even if they were not delusional before. This then becomes a shared psychotic disorder.

Substance Induced Psychotic Disorder – Delusions and hallucinations are common side effects of continuing substance abuse. It can also be a result of withdrawing from an addiction to a substance.

Psychotic order due to a medical condition – A psychotic episode can occur in response to a trauma to the head or an illness, such as a brain tumor that affects the brain. This can cause the sufferer to see, and hear things which are not really there.

Paraphrenia – This is very similar to Schizophrenia but it only occurs in the elderly and starts late in life. The exact reasons why this happens are not yet known.

Both psychotic and personality disorders are included under the broader definition of mental disorders. Whilst there are many similarities between the symptoms and even the treatment of both psychotic and personality disorders there is a fundamental difference in the conditions:

A personality disorder is something which is a manifestation of your personality; it is an extreme of your normal behavior and can be both recognized and treated. Most people with personality disorders are happy to work with medical professionals to live a 'normal' life. They are capable of what is termed as normal function and can integrate into society.

Someone with a psychotic disorder is less likely to be able to function in the normal way expected by society. They are less aware of the expected moral standards and more likely to live inside their own worlds and outside of reality. This lack of belief or knowledge of the expected standards of behavior leave those who suffer from these disorders open to behavior that is not acceptable by society; this might be violent crime or self harm. Of course, not all sufferers exhibit such extreme behavior, but all have the potential to do so.

CHAPTER 3: PERSONALITY DISORDERS

There are many different personality disorders and sufferers can range from displaying a few symptoms to every symptom in the manual. Most disorders will come under one of the following nine, main disorders:

ANTISOCIAL PERSONALITY DISORDER

Antisocial personality disorder is a chronic mental illness in which a person's way of thinking and behaving is destructive and distorted. People with this disorder do not care about the rights or feelings of others, the law, or the consequences associated with their actions. These individuals do not feel remorse and will antagonize and manipulate others for their own ends. They can be particularly harsh and callous when dealing with others and will often break the law as they have no respect for it and others. One significant characteristic of someone with antisocial personality disorder is the lack of guilt or remorse they show for their actions.

It is common for people with this disorder to lie, act on impulse and even behave violently towards others. They often struggle with substance abuse.

The way that individuals with this disorder perceive the world and the people around them, as well as themselves, makes it impossible for them to live a fulfilling life and therefore causes problems with their school, jobs, and families.

Symptoms

There are many symptoms associated with an antisocial personality disorder; it is possible that someone will display all of the symptoms but people can only display a few of the symptoms. Should a diagnosis be necessary it is essential to contact a medical professional for further advice and confirmation. The most common symptoms are:

- No regard for what society defines as right and wrong.
- Constant lying, particularly to exploit others for their own gain.
- Manipulating others via charm and wit, again for their own personal gain or satisfaction.
- Sense of superiority to others and even a touch of exhibitionism.
- Repeatedly in trouble with the law.

- Violating the human rights of others via intimidation, dishonesty or manipulation.
- May have suffered child abuse or neglect when they were young; they are likely to pass this on their own children.
- Hostility; including easily agitated and irritable. They can also be prone to outbursts of violence.
- Lack of ability to feel empathy or regret when dealing with other people; they may appear detached and aloof or distant and uncaring.
- They will be prone to dangerous behavior and taking unnecessary risks as they are oblivious to the consequences.
- Bad attitude towards work and inability to deal with safety concerns at work.
- They do not have the ability to learn from the consequences of any negative behavior.
- Cruelty towards animals or a tendency to bully others.
- Social isolation and poor school performance can be early warning signs of this disorder.

Causes

Antisocial personality disorder is caused by a combination of nature and nurture, or genetics and the environment. Some research hypothesizes that the genetic cause of the disorder comes from dysfunctional genes or hormones, or even a part of the brain. However the general consensus appears to be that the disorder is typically shaped during childhood and then increases in severity over time into adulthood.

Although the exact cause is unknown, there are several risk factors connected with the childhood of sufferers that can increase the chance of someone having the disorder.

Childhood

During childhood, the absence of a parent or abuse in the home can increase the risk of a child growing up to have antisocial personality disorder. A lot of individuals who suffer from this disorder have parents who had substance abuse problems. This makes sense because when a parent struggles with abusing drugs or alcohol they are unable to provide adequate supervision. When a child gets less attention, the parents aren't able to steer the child away from trouble and bad influences. They can also give inappropriate discipline, which is harmful to a child and poses as another risk factor.

Additionally, growing up in a disrupted home increases the risk of antisocial personality disorder. In a disrupted home, no strong bonds are developed and there is a lack of consistent; and appropriate discipline. There is also often a disregard for rules and authority.

Children need strong and positive role models in their lives. Without this, they have a greater chance of getting into trouble at a young age. Child abuse is also linked to antisocial behavior. When a child grows up with neglected and violent parents, abuse becomes a learned behavior.

Diagnosis

When someone is believed to have antisocial personality disorder, there are various medical and psychological tests that professionals do to make an accurate diagnosis.

- The Physical Exam – This is necessary to rule out other causes for the symptoms, like drugs, alcohol, or medical complications.
- Lab tests – It is likely that the doctor will do a blood test to check thyroid levels, blood count and whether there are any substances in the body, such as alcohol or drugs.

- Then, a mental health provider will perform a psychological evaluation to assess a person's feelings, behaviors, relationships, and family history. They will question the individual about their symptoms, the severity of them, and how they affect their ability to live their life. People with antisocial personality disorder are not likely to give accurate answers or accurate information about their symptoms. As previously noted, they are master manipulators. Because of this, professionals will often question the close family and friends of the individual to collaborate the information.

The key in diagnosing personality disorders is examining how the person relates to others. A person with antisocial personality disorder has a superior attitude and cannot relate to people on their level. They feel no remorse for anyone else or their feelings. Along with this, they also don't have any self-awareness of their own feelings either. By speaking to someone for a period of time, it is possible to observe this complete lack of empathy and care for others, depending on how good they are at hiding it. It is also possible to notice the egotistical attitude that many people with this disorder hold.

Like any other disorder, professionals use a set of diagnostic criteria to determine whether or not someone has the disorder. For antisocial personality disorder, there are three criteria that must be met.

1. The person must be at least 18 years old because antisocial personality disorder is not diagnosed in children.

2. The individual must have had at least some symptoms of conduct disorder before age 15. These symptoms could include vandalism, stealing, bullying, violence, or abuse to animals.

3. The sufferer must exhibit a number of symptoms. These symptoms include hostility, risk-taking, breaking the law, always conning or lying to people, being aggressive and assaulting others, showing no remorse or empathy towards others, having no concern for the safety or well-being of others, being impulsive, and being irresponsible when it comes to work and finances.

Treatment

Antisocial personality disorder is one of the most difficult disorders to treat. Most individuals do not want treatment or do not think they need it. The best treatment for this kind of disorder is really based on the individual, their situation, and how severe the symptoms are.

Long-term psychotherapy is a method that is used, but is not always effective. This therapy involves talking about the problems, and the feelings and emotions associated with them. If a person cannot admit to their problems or their symptoms, then this talk therapy approach is ineffective. This type of therapy is often mandated by the courts, especially if the individual is in a jail or prison, they may be required to participate in therapy while they are incarcerated in the hope that this will help them to live normal lives and stay out of trouble.

The therapy focuses on rebuilding relationships and improving their lives once they are released. Professionals also try to talk to the individuals about their disorder and the behaviors and feelings associated with it. Individuals are often unmotivated in these types of settings, but there is still a chance that it can be beneficial.

The goal of therapy used for antisocial personality disorder is to build connections between a person's feelings and their behaviors, because somehow these connections have been lost during their lives.

It is important for the therapist to establish a good sense of trust with the individual. This can be difficult because this disorder doesn't involve very much trust. The relationship the individual builds with the therapist may be their very first relationship, because sufferers of this disorder do not generally have the ability to form positive relationships. Because of this, they may be unwilling to share information or trust the therapist.

The therapy that is given really has to focus on the emotions of the person. Antisocial personality disorder makes individuals numb to their emotions. It's the therapist's job to make them feel these emotions again and then reinforce them.

People with antisocial personality disorder typically do not recognize that there are consequences for their behavior, but they do have to face up to them eventually. Courts and jail time can sometimes be motivating in helping them get treatment and begin to change their behaviors.

There are no medications that are approved to treat antisocial personality disorder and there is no medication that can, but it is possible for some antipsychotics and mood stabilizers to help with some of the symptoms, for example, aggression.

There are treatments and skills courses for the families of the individuals who have antisocial personality disorder. The families are given skills so they can learn how to cope. They also learn how to set boundaries to protect themselves from the violence, anger, and aggression that comes with the disorder.

Individuals with antisocial personality disorder have an increased risk of dying due to violent methods. They also have a great chance of long-term unemployment, homelessness, broken marriages, and frequent prison incarcerations.

PARANOID SCHIZOID

This condition is often seen as starting when a child is as young as three months old. The theory goes that a child can see good and bad but develops an irrational fear that the bad things will destroy them and all the good things. This causes them to be paranoid and often aggressive towards anything they perceive is bad.

The child is likely to grow up socially detached and will avoid intimacy, limit their expression of emotion and even develop an inability to feel pleasure. It is rare for someone suffering from this condition to have strong emotions. They are also unlikely to return any smile or other facial gesture.

One of the issues associated with this disorder is the lack of ability to focus on a goal; people with the condition will often simply drift through life, reacting very little to either adversity or moments of great triumph and happiness; whether in their lives or in the life of someone they know.

Symptoms

There are many symptoms of this disorder; the American Psychiatric Association states that a sufferer should display at least four of the following symptoms:

- Someone who does not desire or enjoy close relationships of any sort. This includes family relationships, being part of a family or engaging in family activities.
- A person who will choose a solitary activity over any sort of group interaction.
- Someone who displays little or no interest in having sexual experiences with another person.
- Someone who never seems to enjoy an activity, no matter what it is.

- A person who does not appear to have any close friends or confidants. The only exception to this is a first-degree relative.
- A person who has no awareness or concern regarding praise or criticism from others.
- Someone who is emotionally cold and appears detached; no matter how severe the trauma. There will also be no emotional response when given flattery or praise of any sort.
- The behavior and emotional response shown by the person must be dramatically opposed to the usual behavioral pattern of the average person brought up in a similar environment and cultural or religious
- This pattern of behavior and attitude towards others must be present in all the sufferer's dealings, whether on a personal or social level, with or without known friends or associates and regardless of the situation they are placed in.
- The deviant attitude and behavior should lead to significant distress or impairment in any social, occupational, or other important areas of functioning.

Causes

Paranoid Schizoid was first mentioned as a disorder in its own right by Melanie Klein, who was following the work done by Freud and Ronald Fairbairn. The belief was that this condition would start at an early age and was generally triggered by the environment around a child. The theory postulated that this condition would be brought about by a difficult start in life which would lead a child to struggle with their own ego and reconciling the good and bad elements of it into a balanced personality.

Those afflicted by this disorder will fragment them self and block out all negative and bad elements. As these elements are fragmented the good parts are kept and form the ego; thereby creating the persona of someone who can do no wrong in their own eyes and is incapable of seeing the harm they can cause others as a bad thing. The fragmented bad elements are cast out of the ego and into the world, discarded and no longer a part of the afflicted person's life.

Other theories regarding the cause of this condition include the idea that a person believes that other people are deliberately deceptive and malicious. This combined with a low level of self confidence to create a paranoid state in the mind; a situation which is reinforced by the activities of others around the sufferer. Someone with this condition will only see what they choose to see and completely ignore positive or life affirming actions which go against the idea formed in their head.

It has also been suggested that paranoid schizoid is a result of a genetic disorder. A defect in the genes can lead to paranoia which is then magnified into paranoid schizoid by the environment around those who suffer from this condition. Research has shown there is a genetic link between those with paranoid schizoid and schizophrenia.

Diagnosis

It may be tempting to self diagnose this condition or even to diagnose it for someone you know. However, it should always be entrusted to a medical professional to confirm any diagnosis. There are many personality disorders which are similar to each other and effective treatment can only be administered if you know which one you are dealing with.

A medical professional will use behavioral records and a carefully composed set of questions to ascertain whether someone is suffering from paranoid schizoid or not. There is currently no scientific test which can confirm a doctor's conclusion; this is why it is essential that a professional, with experience of personality disorders, diagnosis the issue. It is likely that they will also ask the family or any care givers a few questions to verify the response of the sufferer.

It s worth noting, that this condition has been found to be more common amongst biological relatives of someone with schizophrenia.

Treatment

Successful treatment revolves around building a relationship of trust with a physician or therapist. This is essential, and must be established before any discussion or treatment is even thought about. Once the trust has been earned then it needs to be held onto and this can be a difficult process, those with paranoid schizoid are wary of everyone and even those they trust can be seen to be the enemy.

Once the trust is in place a therapist will need to talk to the person regularly and encourage them to talk about issues they had when growing up. It is possible that talking about childhood issues can help the person to be less suspicious and more accepting of other people and their intentions. However, most physicians will agree that this is one of the most difficult of the personality disorders to treat and is a long term commitment.

It can also be beneficial to set small goals for a patient to attempt to reach in between meeting their therapist. These goals will help the patient to focus on something other than their natural paranoia and learn to deal with environments that currently make them uncomfortable.

It is interesting to note that the majority of paranoid schizoid sufferers who seek treatment do so voluntarily.

SCHIZOTYPAL DISORDER

Perhaps one of the biggest challenges someone suffering from schizotypal disorder faces is the inability to establish and maintain a close relationship with another person. Someone who suffers from this disorder will be extremely uncomfortable meeting new people although they may also be anxious to meet 'the one'. They are not deliberately anti-social but their generally eccentric behavior will cause a difference in their perceptions of other people's actions, compared to what the average person sees.

It is for this reason that they will struggle to establish any close relationship. The disorder often manifests itself as an ability to incorrectly interpret any event. A gesture that may appear as a normal social interaction will be taken out of context by someone suffering from this disorder and take on a special meaning. This can often lead to the person coming across as 'creepy' because they are seeing a deeper meaning in everyday actions that those which are actually taking place.

It is common for those who are suffering from this disorder to seek medical assistance for anxiety or depression as they may not realize they have schizotypal disorder.

The Symptoms

There are several symptoms which will appear in those who are suffering from this condition. The underlying issue will probably be linked to the inability of sufferers to form close relationships. There are many social and cultural deficits in the behavioral patterns of people with this disorder:

- Ideas of reference – this is the idea, mentioned above, that simple everyday events and gestures have a deeper meaning than they actually do. This can often be seen in those with this disorder when they expect something from someone, even though the other party is not aware of what is expected of them! This also often manifests as an emotional attachment to someone which is not desired or encouraged.

- A belief in a fantasy or magical ability which influences their behavior as they believe this ability is real. The average member of society would not even entertain the notion that they believe to be true.

- Someone with this disorder is likely to have an unusual amount of perceptual experiences; this may include, although are not limited to bodily illusions.

- Those with this disorder will often have odd speech; they will be overly theatrical or exceptionally vague.

- Suspicion of anyone and everything around them is common in people with this condition; this makes it very difficult to relate to others.

- They are likely to display an inappropriate or constricted affect. This is either a complete lack of emotion or an overly exaggerated emotional response to a given situation.

- People whose behavior is odd or eccentric compared to the socially accepted norm can, potentially have a schizotypal disorder.

- People who suffer from this personality disorder are unlikely to have any close friends; their only confidants will be close family members; people they have grown up with and trust.

- Social anxiety is a normal response for many people when entering a new situation. However, someone with this disorder will retain the social anxiety even if they have become familiar with the situation. This anxiety will usually manifest itself as a paranoid fear of something or someone at the social occasion.

Cause

As with many of the personality disorders current medical research has failed to provide an answer as to what actually causes schizotypal disorder. The general consensus is that it is caused by a combination of genetic makeup, social factors and psychological influences. In short the disorder is a result of your genes, the way you have been brought up, how you interact with others and your personality and temperament.

There is no single, deciding factor, contracting the disorder is a complex result of the interaction of the above factors.

Diagnosis

A personality disorder must be a long term health issue and not something that only affects a person for a few months.

Issues during childhood are often overlooked and dismissed for a variety of reasons; this makes it highly likely that a diagnosis of schizotypal disorder will not be made until someone is in their twenties. It is essential to have had the condition for at least a year before a diagnosis can be made.

A diagnosis is not likely to be possible from your normal family physician; they will need to refer you to a trained and experienced mental health professional such as a psychologist or psychiatrist. It is not possible to diagnose this condition by simply taking blood samples or hormone levels, it must be confirmed by a professional who will ask the appropriate questions regarding your health, attitude towards others and social interactions.

In fact, it is common for those with this disorder to seek health care advice and support for one of the symptoms before talking about the actual disorder. Health care is not usually sought until the disorder causes a significant detrimental effect to someone's ability to work or interact with others.

To be diagnosed with this disorder your symptoms must generally match those described above.

Treatments

The average person with this disorder will distort their version of reality dramatically to the actual reality. This makes it essential for any medical professional to treat their patient with a great deal of care. You should never directly confront or contradict the afflicted person. The best treatment method is to build an atmosphere of trust and support which will allow the sufferer to open up regarding their thoughts and feelings. As someone progresses it may even be possible to introduce the idea of group therapy.

Providing training in social skills and behavioral science can help someone who is suffering from this disorder to learn how to interact with others and create lasting friendships.

Medical treatments are available for any period when a sufferer is experiencing an acute phase of psychosis; these are commonly experienced in times of extreme stress or when particular events have left them feeling unable to cope. Psychosis is usually a temporary part of this disorder; a reaction to a specific stimuli.

As this disorder leaves you feeling naturally suspicious and distrusting of the motivation of others it is unlikely that an online forum or self help group will be of any assistance. It is best to build a relationship of trust with one physician and build on this relationship over time.

BORDERLINE PERSONALITY DISORDER

This personality disorder causes people to have unstable moods and behavior; people who suffer from this condition usually have difficulty in building relationships. The disorder was first recognized in 1980 when it was listed in the Diagnostic and Statistical Manual for Mental Disorders; the third edition of the book which most medical professionals use when diagnosing mental illness.

More severe cases of this disorder will involve temporary psychotic episodes; it was these that prevented the disorder from being recognized in its own right. The psychotic episodes led many doctors to believe that a patient had an atypical version of another personality disorder.

The key issues and challenges facing someone with this disorder are:

- Difficulty in controlling and regulating emotions and thoughts
- A tendency to be reckless and impulsive rather than considering the consequences.

- An inability to form good relationships with others, relationships which are formed are usually unstable.

Anyone who has this disorder has a high probability of having other disorders at the same time. Potential disorders include depression, anxiety, substance or eating disorders and even self-harming disorders.

The Symptoms

As with all personality disorders it is necessary to show that the symptoms have existed over a lengthy period of time, the minimal time period required is one year. For a medical professional to make a diagnosis of borderline personality disorder they will need to see that you display at least five of the following symptoms:

- Extreme reactions to any situation where they may perceive they could be abandoned. Reactions may include rage, panic or depression.
- Relationships with others will be intense and stormy. The relationships will often alter between complete devotion and extreme hate; this can happen in a matter of minutes.

- Someone with this disorder will often have a distorted image of them self. It is also usually an unstable image and can result in sudden changes in their feelings, plans, values or even their goals for the future.
- They will be very impulsive individuals. This is often shown by a spontaneous spending spree or a string of unsafe sexual encounters. Even substance abuse and binge eating can be a result of this impulse.
- Someone with this disorder will display tendencies towards suicide and may have even attempted it in the past. They may also be prone to harming themselves physically.
- Mood swings with a deep intensity becoming apparent for the current mood. Each mood can last from a few hours to a few days.
- Someone with this disorder will frequently feel bored or devoid of any emotion. This is when they can be at their most reckless.
- People with this personality disorder will have problems controlling anger and may have outbursts of intense anger at the most inappropriate times.

- Sufferers can often have out of body experiences where they feel they are observing themselves from outside their body. This can result in them feeling cut off from society. It can also lead to cases of paranoia and a loss of touch with reality.

Any of these symptoms can be triggered by the simplest of things, even things which seem completely innocent to everyone else.

Cause

There has been a limited amount of research into this disorder and there are not yet any conclusive findings regarding the cause of this illness. Scientists do agree that it is likely to be caused by both genetic and environmental factors; in fact, studies involving twins show that there is a high probability that the illness is inherited.

As many personality traits are inherited it is possible that the strongest traits; those of impulsiveness and aggression are key to the development of this disorder. As such the link between the genes which control impulses and regulate emotions are being investigated as potential sources of the disorder.

It is also believed that unstable family relationships will increase the likelihood of contracting borderline personality disorder. Research also suggests that those with this disorder are more likely to become victims of violent crime, including rape. This is because they will often be impulsive rather than considering all the consequences and available actions.

Diagnosis

The best and safest way for this disorder to be diagnosed is by an experienced and well established mental health professional. A physician will provide you with a thorough medical exam; this is not to ensure they are diagnosing you correctly but it will assist in ruling out any other possible diagnosis. The main steps in diagnosing the disorder will be an extensive interview by a health care professional; this will include an in-depth talk about the symptoms.

Women are more likely to have a co-occurring disorder; such as depression or anxiety. Men are more likely to have the disorder complicated by substance abuse or antisocial personality disorder.

It has also been suggested that borderline personality disorder will make someone have a more extreme reaction to the use of an unpleasant word.

Other illnesses, such as diabetes, chronic back pain or high blood pressure are common in those suffering from borderline personality disorder. This is because the medications prescribed can lead to obesity and this leads to the diseases mentioned above.

As with the other personality disorders there is not one single test that a doctor can perform to confirm the presence of the disorder.

Treatments

The best and most successful approach to treating people with this disorder is 'talk therapy'. Research has shown that those who are treated in this manner show positive signs of improvement over a period of time. The main treatment methods are:

- Psychotherapy

This treatment method allows the patient to talk and build a trusting relationship with their therapist. The main target of this approach is enabling the patient to share their experiences and reason them through. Research has shown that this approach is successful in relieving the symptoms of the disorder.

- Cognitive Therapy

This therapy is designed to assist people to identify their core beliefs and learn how to evaluate and change them. The result is a better understanding of yourself and a reduced ability and desire to harm yourself.

- Dialectical Behavior Therapy

The focus of this therapy is to teach people to be aware of the world around them and focus on the current moment. This therapy has been shown to help people control their emotional responses; this helps people to form lasting relationships and accept their beliefs and behavior.

- Schema – Focused Therapy

The focus of this therapy is to change the way people see themselves. The therapy derives from the idea that borderline personality disorder is created by a bad self image which has been created in childhood. This therapy will help people to cope with stress and learn to interact successfully with others.

HISTRIONIC PERSONALITY DISORDER

People who have this disorder will be desperate to be the centre of attention; they will do almost anything to ensure everyone is focusing on them. The condition makes them feel very uncomfortable and emotional should they be sidelined for any reason. Reasons they are sidelined can be as simple as someone else telling the story of their recent holiday; to a person with this disorder this is tantamount to a slap in the face.

The usual reaction to this uncomfortable feeling is to do something extreme to return the attention to them. They are often seen as shallow as they will use sex and seduction as a means to keep the focus on them instead of as a display of love. People with this disorder are often fun to be around, they are lively, incredibly energetic and very interesting; with a huge dramatic streak. However this desire for attention can cause serious issues in their relationships with others.

The desire to be the centre of attention will make it difficult for someone suffering from this disorder to achieve or maintain emotional intimacy within a relationship. This is made more difficult as they will often act out a role; such as a princess or the victim. The acting can be used to emotionally manipulate others and is often in a bid to control a partner; despite the fact that they are also incredibly dependent on their partner for the attention and support they think they need.

The constant need for attention and lack of respect for conventional boundaries will make it difficult for a person with this disorder to build and maintain long lasting friendships. If the attention seeking part of their mind is not satisfied they will often become depressed and withdrawn; they will then use this upset to return the attention to them self.

The desire to be centre of attention will push someone with this disorder to constantly look for new ways to do things or even new things to do; they will desire instant gratification and are likely to struggle to maintain any job as their interests change so quickly. They have an intense dislike for anything routine and will struggle to become part of a long term relationship as there is always something new and more exciting around the corner.

Symptoms

To make a diagnosis of this disorder a medical professional will be looking for the patient to display at least five of the following symptoms and to have had these symptoms for over a year. As with many personality disorders it is unusual to be diagnosed before your twenties.

- The person will display a huge amount of discomfort in any situation where they are not the centre of attention.

- The person suffering from this disorder will often engage in sexually seductive and provocative behavior; particularly when it is not appropriate.
- Their emotions will rapidly change depending upon the scenario and the need to manipulate others. Much of their behavior will be seen to be shallow and selfish.
- They are highly likely to use their own physical appearance to draw attention to themselves. This may be via wearing very provocative clothes or by overdoing a particular style; such as Goth or even punk.
- A person with this disorder is liable to engage in a huge amount of meaningless chatter; but their speech will lack detail and will be their own, impressionistic view of the world around them.
- In order to constantly be the centre of attention people with this disorder are likely to be extremely susceptible to other people's suggestions; particularly if they think it will help them to stay in the limelight. This ability to be easily led means they will often find themselves in a precarious or illegal situation.

- Despite their short attention span, someone with histrionic disorder is liable to consider a relationship between them and someone else to be far more intimate than it actually is; this is in part thanks to their need for attention and partly because of their naturally provocative and sexual nature.

Cause

It is usually possible to diagnose this condition by early adulthood, although there is no scientific explanation for the cause of this illness yet. As with many of the personality disorders research suggests that both genetics and the environment someone is brought up in play a part in the development of this condition.

Children will naturally emulate their parents and research has shown that children whose parents have histrionic disorder are more likely to display the symptoms themselves. This lends credence to both the thought that it is genetically influenced and a product of a person's upbringing.

Diagnosis

The usual path to a correct diagnosis of this condition is to visit your physician regarding one of the symptoms of the condition, such as depression. Your physician will probably conduct medical and physical examinations to eliminate various conditions from a possible diagnosis. When they are unable to find a cause for your illness they will refer you to a mental health specialist.

There is no specific test which will tell you or your physician that you have histrionic disorder. Instead this will be concluded via an in-depth discussion and by monitoring your behavioral patterns.

Treatment

Unfortunately treatment for those with histrionic disorder will revolve around a schedule of meetings with a therapist. This can, in itself, be unappealing to the sufferer as they have a dislike for anything too routine.

The most effective treatment available at the moment is with a psychotherapist; their job is to ensure an afflicted person has the opportunity to discuss their experiences and feelings. This approach can have a high level of success as the sufferer will be the centre of attention whilst being treated.

Through talking and guidance a therapist will encourage someone suffering from this condition to relate to other people positively rather than in an attention seeking way.

Whilst there is no medication available to help with the treatment of histrionic disorder, your physician may provide you with anti-depressants or anti-anxiety pills. This will be to assist during any depressed periods although the pills should be taken with care as they are highly addictive.

NARCISSISTIC DISORDER

The basic premise of this personality disorder is an inflated sense of self worth. This trait is often emphasized by a need to be appreciated and admired although someone with this disorder usually is unable to have any empathy for others; no matter what their situation.

People with this disorder will often be fond of overly grand gestures and will assume they are the most important part of anyone's life; even if you met them just five minutes ago. There are very few scenarios where this inflated sense of self worth is appropriate in modern society. Surprisingly, under this façade there is usually a very fragile self esteem which needs the consistent bolstering of ego that their behavior attracts.

People with this disorder will often appear to be snobbish, disdainful or simply patronizing and condescending. They are likely to give out opinions on the failings of others at the drop of a hat without acknowledging their own shortcomings.

The belief that they should be the most important person in any room can lead to issues when dealing with relationships at home or at work; this will be particularly noticeable if someone else is praised and you are not. In situations such as these, it is common for someone with this disorder to react angrily or impatiently; making it very difficult to build a long term relationship.

The Symptoms

Again, in order for someone to be diagnosed with this condition they will need to display at least five of the following symptoms and to have had these issues for at least one year.

- A sufferer has a hugely inflated opinion of their own self worth. They will usually inflate their achievements and skills to ensure they are the best in the room. They are unlikely to be able to substantiate any of these claims.

- They often indulge in a fantasy world where they have unlimited success, power, money and love. This indulgence can occur at any time.

- They will have a belief that they are very special and that there are only a few other people in the world which are on the same level as them. This belief means they will often try to associate with these people and no one else; as these are the only people who will understand them.

- The belief that they are special necessitates them to expect and demand your praise and adulation at all times of the day. They expect to be admired simply for being who they are. This belief extends to expecting others to provide them with favorable treatment and to know their expectations without being told them.

- This feeling of their own self worth will cause many people with this disorder to take advantage of others in order to achieve their own goal. They are unlikely to see this as exploitation; instead, it is just others doing what they should to satisfy their needs.

- It is usual for someone with this personality disorder to lack empathy towards others, particularly those who they feel are beneath them; which is almost everyone.
- Envy is a common trait in people with this disorder. They are liable to be envious of anyone who has something they do not and they will believe others are envious of them; because of their importance.
- People who suffer from this illness will often come across as arrogant, haughty or even rude.

This disorder occurs in more men than women and current estimates suggest that the disorder is present in approximately six percent of the population. Symptoms associated with this disorder will always be present, even when a child; but the constantly evolving personality is likely to mask this and it is not usually possible to diagnose the condition until the late teens or early twenties.

Cause

It is not yet possible to identify the exact cause of this illness. As with all the personality disorders it is suggested to be a response to both genetic and lifestyle influences. This makes it an incredibly complex disorder to study as every person is subject to different influences during their upbringing, even siblings can be treated very differently and experience life according to their own personality and outlook.

This disorder has been linked to excessive criticism or even excessive pampering during childhood. It is also believed that there is a link between the brain, someone's behavior and the way they think; although research is still ongoing into this.

Diagnosis

Many children will display narcissistic traits as they mature; this is relatively normal behavior and is a necessary part of growing and developing as a person. As a result it is highly unlikely that any child will be diagnosed with narcissistic personality disorder; this is usually something which is discovered when they reach adulthood and seek treatment for a common side effect, such as anxiety (caused by their low self esteem).

To correctly identify this disorder it will be necessary to see a mental health care expert who will ask questions such as:

- How do you feel and act when others criticize you?
- Do you have any close personal relationships?
- How would you describe your childhood?

These questions are used to build a picture of you and your personality and to confirm that your signs and symptoms match those of someone with narcissistic personality disorder.

Physicians tend to take their time when diagnosing a mental illness as many of them have very similar traits; this can make it easy to diagnose incorrectly or to conclude you have several different personality disorders at the same time.

Treatments

Talking is the most important and most effective treatment method for those with this disorder. A psychotherapist will work alongside someone with this disorder for several years, gradually changing their personality and outlook on life.

The primary aim is to teach someone to relate better to others; this will provide the opportunity to build lasting, loving and intimate relationships. It is also essential to work out what drives your emotions and causes you to be competitive or distrusting.

It is essential for anyone with this disorder to learn to accept their own skills and limitations, this will enable them to handle criticism and understand what they can truly achieve.

A therapist will assist them to regulate their feelings and react in a positive manner, whenever possible.

There is currently no medication available to assist with the treatment of this disorder. Although, if you suffer from symptoms of depression; it is possible to obtain medication to assist with treating this.

AVOIDANT PERSONALITY DISORDER

This disorder leaves those suffering from it with exceptionally sensitive natures. They are always concerned with what others think and will be very quick to jump to a negative conclusion. The condition is worsened by a feeling of inadequacy; no matter what situation they find themselves in.

People who have this disorder generally avoid social interactions as they do not feel comfortable, confident or even adequate to be in a social scenario. Their behavior is often typified by the avoidance of social encounters and even their jobs are likely to be independent and isolating.

In a social setting someone with this illness will be tense and probably fearful; this will reinforce their image to others as an easy target and often makes them the target of ridicule. In turn, this ridicule will confirm their own self doubt and complete the vicious cycle. As such, people with this disorder are acutely aware of the movements and expressions of everyone they meet; anxiously looking for signs that they will ridicule them and cause them to blush or cry.

This disorder will often leave people isolated, with few or no confidants which can help them through the rough patches. Despite their personality disorder, people with this disorder are usually desperate for affection and will often fantasize regarding the perfect partner.

As a consequence of avoiding situations where they may meet others they will often suffer in their jobs; either being unable to perform their duties properly due to a lack of interaction or training, or, by missing opportunities for advancement.

Intimate relationships can also be a major issue as it is difficult for someone with this disorder to connect or open up to another human; simply because they will be afraid of being judged. It is very rare for them to speak up in a group scenario, even if they are sure they are correct.

Symptoms

Anyone suffering from avoidant personality disorder will be likely to display most, if not all of the following symptoms:

- An avoidance of any occupational activity which involves a significant amount of contact with other people. This is because of the fear or criticism.
- An unwillingness to communicate and get to know anyone new, unless they can be certain they will be liked.
- Should they form an intimate relationship they will always 'hold back' to avoid the possibility of being ridiculed or embarrassed.
- They are likely to spend much of their time considering the likelihood of rejection or criticism if they are in a social situation. This serves to make any actual encounter worse.
- Will always feel inadequate in a new situation and will, therefore, be unable to present themselves in the best possible light.
- They are likely to see themselves as inferior to others, socially inept and even unappealing to others.

- Will avoid doing anything which could potentially result in an embarrassing situation. It doesn't matter if the activity is risky or not; it is the potential result which causes the problem.

Cause

Again, this personality disorder is thought to be a result of social, biological and genetic factors. It may first appear as a child through signs of excessive shyness and a fear of new people. This should not be confused with a normal child's wariness of meeting new people and an initial shyness which is quite a common reaction.

It is only when this trait continues through the adolescent period and appears in conjunction with a fear of rejection and a high sensitivity to criticism that there becomes a high risk of this disorder developing and being diagnosed in their late teens or early twenties.

It is believed that excessive criticism from a parent and incidents of rejection can be the start of the process which ends in avoidant personality disorder.

Diagnosis

The symptoms of avoidance personality disorder will present themselves to a varying degree in almost everyone at some point in their lives. To be diagnosed with this disorder it is necessary to display these symptoms for an extended period of time and for them to be having a profound effect on someone's ability to live their life.

A diagnosis can only be given and confirmed by a mental health professional. The disorder displays several similarities to schizoid and schizotypal disorders, the main difference being that someone suffering from avoidance personality disorder wants to form relationships but is scared to try.

Again, medical tests will be carried out to rule out any alternative diagnosis and the medical professional will need to ask a wide range of questions to ensure they can make the correct diagnosis.

Treatment

A psychotherapist is the principle form of treatment for this disorder. Sessions with this professional will centre on improving the patient's self-esteem and confidence. As these traits of the personality become stronger, those with this disorder will be better able to deal with criticism and even rejection.

Treatment sessions will start by building a relationship and trust between a patient and the therapist; this will enable the patient to open up without fear of rejection. Practical exercises will be used to highlight the self worth of an individual and heighten their feeling of self esteem.

As the treatment continues, group therapy is often used to encourage them into a larger social gathering; although in this case it is a careful controlled environment.

It is also possible to have monoamine oxidase inhibitors prescribed which will help alleviate feelings of social unease and reinforce successful social encounters.

DEPENDENT PERSONALITY DISORDER

The overriding concern for people suffering from this disorder is that those they love will abandon them. They have a need to be taken care of; emotionally and physically. The behavior of someone suffering from this disorder will modify overtime to become submissive and dependent; effectively forcing others to give them the care that they seek. To people without an understanding of this illness the person will appear 'clingy'.

The longer this scenario continues the more reliant an individual will become and the more they will fear separation and being alone; they will develop a fear that they cannot survive without the help of their chosen loved ones.

A common trait in people with this disorder is pessimism and self doubt, they lose faith in their own ability to do or achieve anything and will often refer to themselves as stupid. Anyone who criticizes their achievements is effectively confirming their belief that they are worthless.

The reliance on others for direction and emotional support will, overtime, severely limit their ability to function on their own and live a normal life. It also becomes difficult to build new relationships as they are already dependent on a few chosen people. People with this disorder often become anxious when forced to make a decision and will avoid any responsibility if possible.

People with this disorder are also very vulnerable to manipulation; they are likely to go along with anything, regardless of whether they believe it to be right or wrong. They will do this to avoid the risk of losing the assistance of their care giver. It is highly unlikely that a person with this disorder will start anything under their own initiative.

Symptoms

The fear of being left alone and the associated 'clingy' behavior will be obvious by the time someone becomes an adult. People who suffer from this illness are likely to display the following traits:

- An inability to make basic, every day decisions, such as the right shirt to wear. The decision will be impossible without a huge amount of reassurance from the right person.

- A need for other people to accept the responsibility for all major areas of their life. This is likely to include telling them which job to do, which neighbors to befriend and even what car to drive.

- Someone with this disorder is unlikely to disagree with other people's opinions, particularly if that person is one of their primary care givers. They would not want to risk losing their care and support.

- They will be very unlikely to start any new project as they lack the self-confidence to believe it is a worthwhile task.

- People with this illness will often go to extreme lengths, including volunteering for very unpleasant jobs; just to ensure they will receive the nurturing and support they crave.
- They will be visibly uncomfortable and probably feel helpless if they are left alone; this is due to their belief that they are physically unable to look after themselves. They worry that they will be abandoned and unable to cope.
- Should a relationship end for any reason, they will urgently look for a new relationship, in which they can depend on a new care giver figure.
- They will spend far too much time worrying about the risk of being left alone to fend for themselves; it may preoccupy any spare time they have.

Cause

As with the majority of personality disorders it is not yet known exactly what causes someone to have a dependent personality disorder. Again, it is believed to stem from social, genetic and biological factors.

Many researchers believe that it starts in childhood and is often the result of either excessive separation anxiety; possible reinforced by periods of separation. Or, that it is a result of an over protective upbringing. This is potentially the case in those that are already prone to the disorder, an over reliance on one or both parents can be continued into adult life. This will often result in the child remaining dependent on their parents long after they have become an adult.

It is also possible that the disorder can be triggered by a one off incident of trauma which may even leave the person temporarily dependent on others. This effect can continue long after the temporary need has abated and result in a fear of being alone and unable to cope; leading to dependent disorder.

Treatment

It is unlikely that someone will seek medical advice for this disorder. It is more common for either the care giver to seek assistance or the sufferer to seek medical assistance for one of the symptoms of the illness. People who suffer from this disorder are often anxious at the thought of a care giver leaving or depressed at what the future may hold. It is these traits that are usually brought to the attention of a physician for treatment, before the personality disorder can be diagnosed.

As with so many personality disorders, the best course of treatment is to use the services of a psychotherapist. The obvious goal of the sessions will be to increase a sufferer's independence and become more active within their community or workplace; increasing their ability to build normal relationships.

A therapist will set short term targets and goals and focus on them with the patient. Setting long term goals will risk transferring of dependency from the current care giver to the therapist and will not be beneficial. Therapists may also seek the assistance of the patient's loved ones who will be able to slowly limit the amount of help they provide whilst continuing to provide emotional support.

Medication is an option to treat the symptoms of dependent personality disorder; these are mainly depression and anxiety. As with any drug it is essential to monitor this carefully to avoid a dependence on the drug forming.

The goal of all treatment is to encourage a person to not only live independently but to learn how to adjust their living habits and behavior to ensure they do not become dependent again in the future.

ANAKISTIC PERSONALITY DISORDER

This personality disorder is also known as Obsessive Compulsive Personality Disorder (OCPD). It is a surprisingly common condition and revolves around the need for orderliness and perfection in every detail. People with this disorder will want mental and interpersonal control over every aspect of their lives; this will almost always be at the expense of flexibility, spontaneity and possibly efficiency.

People who suffer from this illness are likely to become angry very easily when confronted by a situation that they cannot control. This anger is often misdirected, instead of complaining about poor service they will focus on whether to leave a tip or not. Sometimes this anger may explode from within them, with righteous indignation but over a seemingly minor matter.

A common issue for those with this disorder is which decision to make. Should an answer not be immediately apparent in keeping with established rules and procedures. Then it will become an incredibly time consuming task deciding the right path to choose. It is common to spend so long deliberating over the best or most important task that no task ever gets started!

Someone who suffers from this illness will probably be very concerned with their own status in a dominant / submissive relationship; of any sort. It is common for them to defer excessively to someone they respect whilst being especially resistant to anyone they do not respect.

It is also common for someone with anankastic disorder to be stilted or highly controlling when expressing their emotions; particularly in public. They tend to bring a formal air to any relationship and may appear stiff in a social setting where others will be happy to display their emotions. They generally prefer to wait and express the perfect sentiment; their primary focus is logic and intellect as opposed to emotion.

Symptoms

To be diagnosed with this disorder it is necessary to display at least four of the following symptoms and to have displayed them for over a year:

- Being so occupied with the rules, details, organization and arranging the schedules that the whole point of the activity is missed. In fact the whole activity is often missed.

- An inability to complete a project unless it is perfect. This means perfect by their own standards; something which is never really achievable.

- Despite their inability to complete a project they will be completely devoted to work and to the improvement of productivity. This will be to the detriment of any other person or activity.

- Someone with this disorder will have exceptionally high moral standards and will be completely inflexible when it comes to changing their opinion. They will have a very high conscience, particularly in response to ethical matters or their own personal values.

- A person with this illness will not be able to discard any item; whether it has a sentimental value or not and regardless of whether it has a practical use.

- They are highly unlikely to delegate any task to someone else unless they are assured that the task will be carried out using the same method and standards as they, themselves would use.

- They are unlikely to be short of money as they are exceptionally prudent, to the point of being miserly.

Money is seen as something that should be kept for the future; in case it is needed.

- They are incredibly stubborn and it is very difficult to change their mind; no matter how big or small the problem.

It should be noted that OCPD is not the same as Obsessive Compulsive Disorder; which is marked by an obsession with cleanliness and the need to perform rituals before undertaking certain tasks. OCPD is a dedication to perfection; at a level which is rarely, if ever possible.

Cause

It has been suggested by the International OCD Foundation that one in one hundred people have OCPD; it has also been shown to affect twice as many men as it does women.

Whilst the exact cause is not yet clear, there has been a link established between contraction of the disorder and family relationships. This has been evidenced by the number of cases of OCPD which run in a family, clearly confirming that genetics play a part in this disorder.

However, the theory that environmental factors also play a part holds considerable credence for the same reason. Parents who expect perfection from their children will often impose a set of strict rules which must be adhered to. The child will learn to adhere to the rules and take this philosophy into their adult life; already keen to stick to the rules and create a perfect environment.

As with the majority of personality disorders, the way someone is brought up will have an effect on what they perceive to be normal behavior and will, to some extent, be the way they choose to live their life; they know no other way!

Diagnosis

Just as with the other personality disorders described in this book it is essential to visit a physician to have physical tests and blood tests completed; this will rule out many illnesses. It will then be necessary to be referred to a mental health professional for further tests and a diagnosis.

Mental health experts are trained to ask the right questions and to put any patient at ease; ensuring their answers are honest and open. As many of the personality disorders have similar symptoms they will ask as many questions as they need to; in order to confirm the right diagnosis is made.

A professional will take into account your behavior, how long it has affected you and your life / medical history.

Treatment

It is possible that someone suffering from this disorder will be given Selective Serotonin Reuptake Inhibitors (SSRI); these tablets will reduce the ability to complete detail orientated thinking and will improve the flexibility of any patient. This disorder does not usually lead to clinical depression and the use of anti-depressants will not be warranted.

Most people who suffer from this condition will be referred to a therapist. They will arrange regular meetings to discuss the condition and the best methods to address it. Therapists are able to talk to people with this disorder in a reasonable way as they remain fairly balance individuals; with overly perfectionist streaks.

Learning to understand their behavior and how it affects others is the first step towards changing the habits of a lifetime. A psychotherapist will provide this insight and the tools needed to ensure a sufferer places less emphasis on work matters and more on family, home life, personal relationships and leisure time.

Many people with this disorder have high levels of stress and have a constant feeling of urgency. A therapist will teach them to use specific relaxation techniques to decrease these feelings and make them more controllable in the future.

Of all the personality disorders possible this one is felt to have the best chance of recovery and many sufferers can lead a normal, balanced life; providing they adhere to the teachings provided by their therapist!

CONCLUSION

Mental illness is very serious and personality disorders, specifically, can cause serious impairment of functioning in individuals. Thankfully, it is possible to treat, manage, and go further in life even with a non-curable disorder.

There is often a stigma associated with mental illness. This stigma makes us think that individuals who suffer from mental illness are somehow broken. The stigma makes us view mental illness as a weakness. When we create this stigma, we also create self-stigmatization. People with mental illnesses are then made to believe that they are somehow inferior to everyone else around them. They feel shame, embarrassment, isolation, and discrimination.

Creating these kinds of feelings only begins a downward spiral. These feelings of shame and embarrassment can prevent individuals with mental illness from admitting their symptoms and problems. This can hinder them from getting the treatment that they need to have. Additionally, family and friends can have a stigma associated with them that even makes them ashamed or embarrassed. All of this shame causes individuals and their families to conceal or hide the mental illness. This secrecy acts as a barrier or an obstacle to the treatment of the disorders.

Discrimination will result in negative effects for the person who is being discriminated against. Some of the harmful effects of stigma on mental illness include bullying, violence, lack of understanding, fewer work and school opportunities, a reluctance to find treatment, and a personal belief that they will never be able to improve their life or situation. These effects can be very destructive to someone who is already struggling with an illness. Luckily, there are many ways that they can learn to cope.

The most important advice for anyone suffering from a mental illness is to get treatment at the earliest possible stage. This is not always easy as many people do not believe there is anything wrong with them; even if they are told they are not well they may go onto a stage of denial. Once they accept that they do have an illness, it is essential to consult a specialist, acknowledge the disorder and accept the treatment offered.

There will be plenty of people who will attempt to belittle or humiliate you because you have an illness, they are ignorant of the facts and are actually responding to their own fear and stereotyping; this can lead to a sufferer doubting themselves. It is important that anyone with a mental illness does not view their illness as a personal failure or a sign of personal weakness, because it isn't.

It is also very important for anyone suffering from a disorder to educate themselves and learn as much as they can about the condition; this will place them in the best position to benefit from the treatment being offered.

It is crucial that people diagnosed with a personality disorder do not isolate themselves. It can be hard for people with mental illness to talk to others about it, especially when the stereotype says they should be ashamed. But, it is beneficial to talk to people about the illness to get support and encouragement from others.

It is also helpful to remember that a personality disorder does not define who they are; rather than saying, "I am schizophrenic" or "I am bipolar", they should learn to say "I have schizophrenia" or "I have bipolar disorder." This will ensure they keep their identity separate from their disorder.

Something that everyone should try to do, when the opportunity arises, is to speak out against stigma and stereotyping. By speaking out, everyone can help to encourage others who struggle with mental illnesses, as well as educate those who do not.

One final factor which is essential to the treatment of anyone with a personality disorder, is to ensure that family members and loved ones are aware of the situation and how they can support the sufferer. This will be the support group that the person with the disorder turns to when needed and they should all be aware of what the disorder involves and when they should or shouldn't intervene.

For those who struggle with mental illness, it can make a very big difference to accept your condition and learn about it. When people create stigmas and make judgments, they do so without having any understanding of the issue; in fact, many of these stigmas and stereotypes arise from a fear of the unknown. This can be overcome by ensuring that those with the disorder recognize for themselves what they can do to treat the disorder and gain knowledge about it.

It is through knowledge and understanding that anyone will have the ability to both improve their own destiny and help others to enjoy a better quality of life. This is the real key to improving their lives and the lives of others, effectively making the world a better place.

Made in the USA
Lexington, KY
12 February 2016